Contents

What is a river?

Rivers are bodies of mostly **fresh water** that flow to the sea. They can be very different from each other: some rivers flow quickly, others more slowly. Some are narrow streams; others are so wide that you cannot see from one side to the other. A river may be all of these things at different places along its route or at different times of year.

Rivers are often beautiful. They are great for kayaking and other water sports.

Rivers are homes for animals and plants. They are important to people, too. We travel on them; we build towns on their **banks**; we take fish from them for food and we use their water in all sorts of ways.

Kingfishers build their nests in river banks and feed on freshwater fish.

In this book you will find out about rivers: how they change as they flow to the sea and about their incredible power when they flood the land.

Record-breaking rivers

The longest river in the world is the River Nile in Africa (right). It is 6,695 kilometres long and flows through nine countries. The shortest river is the D river, in Oregon, USA. It is just 37 metres long – the length of seven canoes.

The river's course

A river's beginning is called its **source**. From there, the river flows downhill on its journey to the sea. The whole journey from start to finish is called the river's course.

Rivers start in different ways. This one is starting high in the mountains. This part of the river is called its source.

The river moves fast as it flows downhill.

The river gets bigger as other rivers and streams join it.

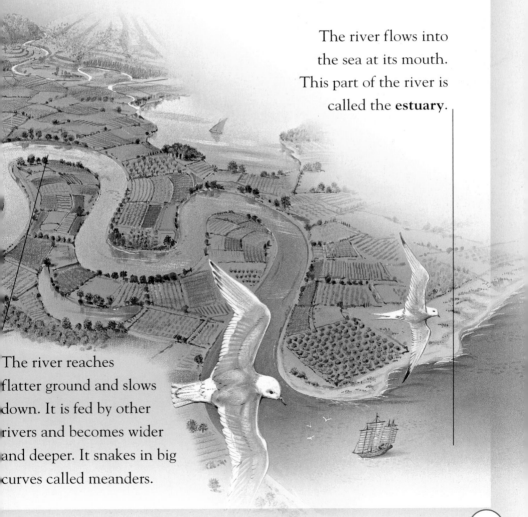

The river's mouth

Rivers carry a lot of mud, which sinks down around the mouth of the river. The mud makes a great feeding ground for birds. They push their beaks into the mud and pull out snails, worms and other juicy creatures.

The river flows into the sea at its mouth. This part of the river is called the **estuary**.

The river reaches flatter ground and slows down. It is fed by other rivers and becomes wider and deeper. It snakes in big curves called meanders.

The water cycle

The water on our planet is constantly being **recycled**. It is always moving between the sea, the air and the land. This movement is called the **water cycle** and rivers are an important part of it.

2. Water vapour rises up into the sky, where the air is colder.

1. The water cycle starts with the Sun. Its heat changes water on the surface of the land and sea into a gas, called **water vapour**.

Recycled water

The water cycle has recycled the same water around our planet for billions of years. So the water you drink today may once have been a drink for a dinosaur, sipping at a river!

3. The vapour turns back into droplets of water, which form clouds.

4. The droplets in the cloud join together and fall as rain.

5. The rain runs into rivers. They carry the water back to the sea, where the cycle starts again.

Shaping the land

Rivers follow the shape of the land but they can also change it. Moving water is very powerful. As a river flows over the land, it picks up stones and even boulders. These roll along with the water. They carve the riverbed and chip at the banks, making the river deeper and wider. This carving and chipping is called **erosion**.

This river in New Zealand is flowing so rapidly it can move boulders.

Sometimes a river flows over a cliff that it cannot wear away. The water tumbles over the rock, making a waterfall.

Victoria Falls, in Africa

On **limestone** hills, rainwater soaks down through the rock. The water drains into underground rivers, which erode tunnels and caves.

The Grand Canyon

Over 3-6 million years, the Colorado river in Arizona, USA, carved a deep **valley** out of solid rock. The valley, called the Grand Canyon, is 365 kilometres long and up to 29 kilometres wide.

River plants

Rivers make good **habitats** for plants because plants need water to grow. Trees that grow alongside rivers have long roots to grip the soil. This helps to hold the river bank together and stops it being washed away.

Trees grow along a river in a rainforest in Malaysia.

Some plants grow mostly under the surface of the water, in places where the river flows very slowly. Others, such as reeds, have their roots under the water but their leaves grow up into the air above.

Giant water lilies have underwater roots. Their huge leaves float on the surface and are up to 2 metres wide!

Plants are important to the life of the river. Their leaves give off a gas called oxygen, which fish and other river life need to breathe. Plants also provide food for animals and safe places to nest or hide.

Spreading seeds

Many plants rely on rivers to spread their seeds. **Tropical** vines, called lianas, drop their seeds into rivers. The seeds float **downstream** to the sea and often sprout on distant shores.

Reeds make perfect nests for water birds.

Animals of the river

Rivers are good habitats for animals. They are home to many kinds of fish, and amphibians such as frogs and newts. In tropical countries, where the climate is warm, there are reptiles such as terrapins and turtles, crocodiles and snakes.

Smaller creatures, such as snails, shrimps, beetles and worms, also live in the river. Many insects, such as dragonflies, live in the water for the first stage of their life. Later, they change into adults, and leave the water for a life in the air.

Frog

Ducks

Beetle

Shrimp

Newt

The otter

Otters are rarely seen because they are shy and **nocturnal** animals. Sometimes you find their droppings, which contain fish bones and scales, and have a very fishy smell.

The river bank is home to mammals and birds. Water voles nest in holes in the banks. Water birds dabble for plants, while otters and kingfishers hunt for fish.

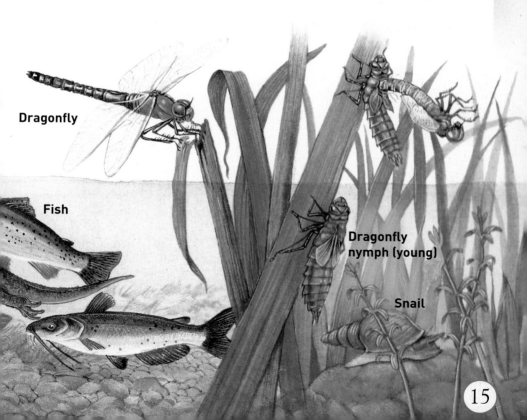

Dragonfly

Fish

Dragonfly nymph (young)

Snail

Rivers and people

People have always lived next to rivers. Many of the world's oldest and most important cities were built on river banks: Cairo is on the River Nile; Rome is on the Tiber and London is on the River Thames.

Riverside towns and cities have lots of bridges so people can cross the water. In New York City, USA, a famous bridge called the Brooklyn Bridge links the city to the town of Brooklyn, on the other side of the East river. This has helped the city to grow.

Thousands of people who live in Brooklyn cross the bridge every day to work in New York's city centre.

Hundreds of people bathe in the River Ganges at Varanasi, India. This town is an important place for Hindus.

Some rivers have a special meaning for people. The Ganges river in India is **sacred** to **Hindus**, who believe it washes away their sins. During certain festivals, millions of **pilgrims** travel to the Ganges to bathe in the water.

Using river water

We use the water from rivers in many different ways. In our homes we use it for drinking, washing, flushing the toilet and watering plants.

Watermills

Watermills have been used on river banks for thousands of years. The rivers turned waterwheels. The waterwheels turned heavy stones, which ground grain into flour. This painting shows a watermill over 600 years ago.

Factories use huge amounts of water. They use it to make things, and to cool down machinery when it gets too hot. Farmers use water, too. They take it directly from rivers to give to their animals and **irrigate** their **crops**.

This big machine is irrigating the crops all around it.

The demand for water is growing and rivers are in danger. If we take too much water from them, river habitats begin to decline and fewer animals live in them. This affects other animals and people, who rely on rivers for food.

Rivers and floods

When a river is very full, it overflows and floods the land. This happens when snow suddenly melts, or heavy rain falls quickly. The river cannot hold all the water, so it bursts its banks.

Sudden floods are dangerous. They destroy buildings and crops, and people and animals may drown. In many parts of the world people try to prevent flood damage. They build barriers such as **dams** and **dykes**, which hold back the water.

In 2011, heavy rains in Thailand caused dangerous floods. Thousands of people had to leave their homes.

These farmers in Thailand are planting rice in flooded fields.

Some rivers flood every year and this can be useful for farmers. In India, China, Thailand and many other countries, rice farmers rely on rivers to flood their rice crops. The water keeps the rice plants cool, and controls weeds and pests.

River Nile

In ancient Egypt, the River Nile flooded every year. This was very important as the water and the **fertile** mud helped crops to grow. Good **harvests** helped Egypt and its people to prosper.

Dams and water power

Rivers flow at different rates throughout the year. In wet seasons, they get so full that sometimes they burst their banks. In dry seasons, they may dry up and disappear altogether. We can control the flow of water by building dams.

A dam is a huge and very strong wall. When one is built across a river, it stops the water flowing forwards. A big lake called a **reservoir** collects behind the dam. This stores fresh water, which is piped to people to use.

The Hoover Dam is on the Colorado river in the USA.

The stored water can also be used to make electricity. When water is released through tunnels in the dam, the force of the water spins machines called turbines. These drive **generators** that make electricity. A quarter of the world's electricity is made from water power.

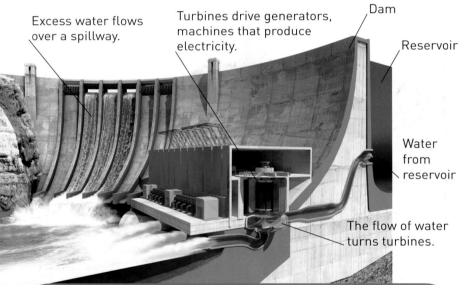

Excess water flows over a spillway.

Turbines drive generators, machines that produce electricity.

Dam

Reservoir

Water from reservoir

The flow of water turns turbines.

Problems with dams

When a new dam is built, people have to leave their homes to make way for the reservoir. Animals and plants lose their habitats, too. When the Aswan dam was built across the River Nile in Egypt, about 200,000 people lost their homes.

River transport

The longest rivers cross countries and continents.
They are useful for travelling along and have
helped people to explore new places.

Rivers are also useful for transporting goods.
The River Rhine passes through six countries
as it flows towards the North Sea. Huge barges
like the one above move up and down the river
to factories along its banks. They supply the
factories with materials, such as steel and coal,
and collect and carry their goods to **port**.

A cruise ship on the Yangtze river in China waits for passengers.

Riverboats come in many shapes and sizes. Small ferries carry people across the river. In cities, pleasure boats take tourists to get a good view of the sights. Giant cruisers are like hotels: they carry people along the river for a few days at a time.

River explorers

About 200 years ago, two explorers, called Lewis and Clark, travelled over 12,500 kilometres across America along rivers to the Pacific coast. Their discoveries tempted people to move home and farm the land.

Enjoying the river

Many rivers are beautiful places where people can relax and have fun. In places where the water flows slowly, people enjoy swimming or boating. In places where the river flows swiftly, kayaking is an exciting river sport.

On warm days, a river's leafy banks are a good place for a stroll or a picnic. If you are lucky, you might spot a kingfisher.

Many people enjoy fishing in rivers. Trout and salmon are delicious to eat, but most people catch fish for sport, not food. If they catch a fish, they quickly free the hook and return the fish to the water.

Dragon boat races

Many boat races take place on rivers. Dragon-boat racing started in China but has now spread all over the world. Each boat contains up to 20 pairs of rowers and a person who strikes a drum. The rowers have to pull the oars in time with the beating drum.

Adding dirty water to rivers harms plant and animal life.

Looking after rivers

Rivers are easily polluted. Factories pour their waste into them or pump warm water into them after using it to cool machines. The waste contains harmful chemicals and the warm water is low in oxygen. Both can harm river life.

How to help rivers

- Save water whenever you can: turn off the tap when you brush your teeth; collect and use rainwater to water plants instead of tap water.

- Join a wildlife group. Local groups visit rivers and report **pollution**.

- Don't drop litter. Litter blows about in the wind and often ends up in rivers.

River clean-ups

Every year in the USA there is a national river clean-up.

All over the country, thousands of people, including children, help to clean up local rivers and streams. Since the clean-ups began over 20 years ago, nearly one million people have taken part and over 900 tonnes of rubbish have been removed from the water.

Farmers also pollute rivers. They use **fertilizers**, which wash into rivers when it rains. This causes water plants to grow very fast. The plants upset the balance of the river and stop sunlight from entering the water.

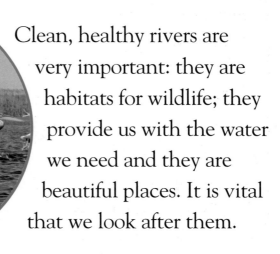

Clean, healthy rivers are very important: they are habitats for wildlife; they provide us with the water we need and they are beautiful places. It is vital that we look after them.

Glossary

banks The sides of a river.

crops Plants grown by farmers for food.

dams Walls built across rivers to hold back the water.

downstream In the direction that a river flows, towards the sea.

dykes Low walls, often made of earth, that are built to prevent flooding.

erosion The removal of soil and pieces of rock on Earth's surface by water, wind or ice.

estuary The place where a river meets the sea.

fertile Fertile land is where plants grow well.

fertilizers Chemicals added to soil to make it more fertile.

fresh water Water in rivers, lakes and ice that is not salty like the sea.

generators Machines that convert movement energy into electrical energy.

habitats The places where particular animals and plants live.

harvests Crops when they are ripe and have been picked.

Hindus Followers of the Hindu religion.

irrigate Water the land.

limestone A type of rock.

nocturnal Awake and active at night.

pilgrims People on a journey to a sacred place.

pollution Harmful waste that damages or poisons the environment.

port A town or city with a harbour.

recycled Used again or made into something new.

reservoir A lake where water is stored for use.

sacred Special or holy to people of a particular religion.

source The place where a river starts.

tropical Belonging to the tropics – warm, wet areas of the world.

valley An area of low land between hills or mountains.

water cycle The movement of water between the Earth's air, the sea and the land.

water vapour Water when it has turned into an invisible gas in the air.

Index